Real Feelings

Heaven on Earth

Brother Bob

Really Feel!

Orangevale, California 1996

Real Feelings

CorelDraw! graphics were used in the book design.

Printed in the United States of America

Publisher's Cataloging in Publication

Bob, Brother.
Real feelings, heaven on earth / Brother Bob.
p. cm.
Preassigned LCCN: 95-71962
ISBN: 0-9644021-3-0

I, Title.

PS3552,O3R43 1996 813'.54
QBI95-20695

E-Mail: bob@bobwayman.com

Dedication

Dedicated to The Presence of Love
—The essence of who we really are.

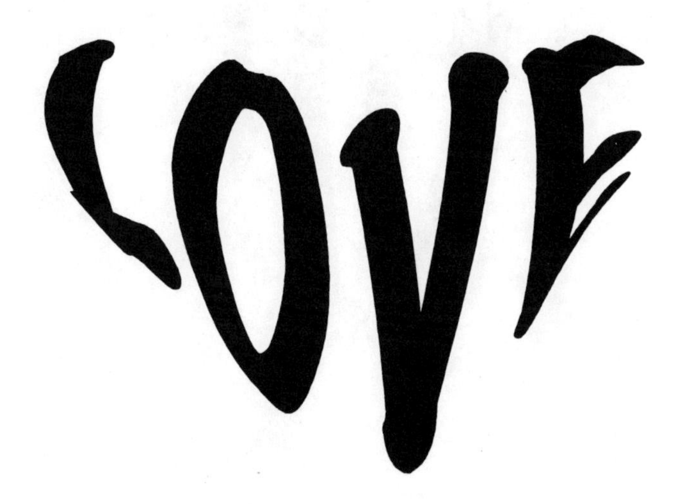

Thank you, Cari, for being my very
loving friend, wife and companion!

TRUTH

Real Feelings

♦ The Repressed Memory

It was a lazy summer afternoon in 1995 in Sacramento, where resting under an oak tree was appropriate. The birds that were chirping in the trees and the sound of the water splashing into the pond from our waterfall were just about ready to put me to sleep. The reverie was broken when I found myself engulfed in a very bright light. I was startled to see a beautiful young woman standing before me. She was so familiar to me, but I could not recall how I knew her.

In the very next moment she said, "Does Astrid ring a bell in your awareness?"

My mind raced back to that May afternoon in 1954, when I was returning home from Lowell Trade High School in Lowell, Massachusetts. That one May afternoon was completely erased from my awareness until Astrid spoke to me. Her voice reconstructed a deeply repressed memory of forty-one years.

How could I have repressed that experience? As I started to remember what had happened that one afternoon, I recalled her words that foretold of this moment.

My mind was on graduation from high school and what I was going to do after that. Was I going to join the U.S. Air Force, or was I going to become an apprentice electrician?

As those thoughts were running through my head, I suddenly became aware of being completely surrounded in a shaft of very bright light. It was as if I was momentarily frozen in this light. This shaft of light seemed to pull me up as if I was riding an elevator into a most peculiar-looking aircraft. I thought that I must have hit my head on something and was hallucinating or I had just had a heart attack and died.

♦ Astrid

As I entered the "aircraft," I was greeted by the most beautiful woman that I have ever seen. She said that her name was Astrid and she would be my "teacher of joy." The subject of joy was not an elective at my school.

I was willing to do anything she said because her eyes evoked a peace that I had never felt before. My initial fear vanished before this incredible source of love.

Astrid appeared to be in her early twenties, although she seemed timeless. She looked exactly the same the second time I saw her as she did the first time we met. Her features were those of a human being except that she exhibited a quality of a more ideal form. She wore a glowing white "dress" covering what appeared to be a body of light. Astrid's hair was iridescent, yet golden. Her eyes were indescribable but hypnotic. They made me remember more than I thought I knew.

Her hands moved with the grace and expression of a hula dancer. Each movement was poetic and purposeful. If she wanted to, I bet she could transform the world with just a few movements. Whenever Astrid laughed, she would fade out of my vision for a few moments. When I asked her about that, she indicated that real laughter actually stopped the world. That may sound a little strange, but somehow I knew what she meant.

This "craft" appeared to be nothing more than pulsating light waves that just faded in and out of my awareness. Nothing about it could be pinpointed as anything describable to be compared to anything else in my memory.

There appeared to be some others onboard; however, they seemed to fade into the background to give Astrid center stage. Every once in a while I would get a glimpse of another being. I did not hear any sounds in this aircraft. In fact, the quietness was almost eerie. While there was some movement, the sounds normally associated with activity were absent from my awareness. The atmosphere was surreal, yet somehow, it was very appropriate.

Even though I refer to this as an aircraft, it was not an aircraft or spaceship in the usual sense—I just do not know what else to call it. I have seen many of the science-fiction movies since that experience, but nothing has come close to this craft in design or appearance.

"Are you from another world?" I inquired.

"Not in the sense that is familiar to you," Astrid offered.

She said that she was where I was, but that her energy vibration was different from what I was normally experiencing. Astrid indicated that my vibrational energy was changed for this encounter.

"Since there is only this *Oneness*, everything can only be happening at the same moment and in the same place," she said.

Astrid went into a long discussion about simultaneous existence at different rates of vibration. Apparently, life is happening all around us outside of our conscious awareness.

Sometimes when we see flickers of light, it could just be an appearance of some other "life-form" communicating with us at a level outside of our conscious awareness. The information is communicated, but we may just have a sense that we had a flash of inspiration, intuition, or a bright idea. The expression, "bright idea," seems most appropriate for these flickers of light.

Even though there is only *here,* the rate of vibration seems to speed up or compress what we call time. Since there is only this present moment called *Now*, everything that happens can only happen in this same moment. This is more fully appreciated when viewed from a higher rate of vibration. Our vibration is almost slow motion, which may give the impression that everything is not connected. Oneness is clearly experienced once we get in harmony with the awareness of our *Real Self.*

My questioning just about covered everything one could imagine asking. "Am I really dead? Is this heaven? Are you an angel?" I was absolutely certain that it could not be hell—not that I did not deserve to be in hell, if such a place existed.

She just smiled at me. Her smile could make anyone forget fear or anything else. Astrid immediately put me at ease.

She said that our encounter would be brief. In the "time of the world" it would not take any time. She saw my puzzled look and assured me that it all would be made clear. I thought that it had something to do with the compression of time due to different rates of vibration. Since then I have learned that the key word is "time."

"Why was I chosen for this experience?" I wondered. Astrid said that I had a very special function to perform in "time," but I would not consciously remember any part of this meeting for at least forty years.

She laughed when I said, "In forty years, I probably will be too old to remember anything." She then reassured me that I would remember everything at our next encounter when she would appear and say, "Does Astrid ring a bell in your awareness?" That statement was a powerful hypnotic suggestion. I bet that the great hypnotherapist, Doctor Milton Erickson, would have been pleased with the ease in which Astrid could induce relaxation.

Astrid beckoned me to be seated across from her. It was very difficult not to stare at her beauty, so I delighted in hanging on to her every word in rapt attention.

"We will begin this very moment to rearrange your perception," Astrid so softly whispered.

"I don't know what that means," I replied.

"Oh, you will, and your focus will be flawless," she responded. "Your gift is the mirroring of Reality by seeing It everywhere. You will not even have to say anything for it to be reflected."

"When will I ever understand any of this in order to have this awareness?" I wondered aloud.

"Your understanding is really not required to *Know* what it is to *Know*," she answered.

She said that I was already aware of what I was really capable of *Knowing*, except that I just chose not to remember that *knowing* awareness at this particular moment.

♦ Patience

Astrid told me that my lifetime on Earth would cover all of the usual adventures of what might be considered the ordinary person. Then my awareness would be jolted by what I would probably consider some very extraordinary experiences. The awareness from these experiences will lead me into the full awareness of *Self*.

"Can I have some of these experiences now so I can be prepared for what is to come?" I requested.

"Patience is something you may be struggling with for many years to come," she foretold. "When you are ready for patience, it will be in your next heartbeat," she claimed.

Apparently, I had decided to experience being impatient so I would be able to see beyond the idea of any impatience in another, as well as to appreciate acceptance and the peace inherent in patience.

In 1993, I started to have these extraordinary experiences that Astrid foretold. Even though they had a profound effect on me, I did not associate any of those experiences at the time with this encounter with Astrid. As far as I could tell, Astrid was never in my conscious awareness.

I guess repressed memories can stay buried for a very long time. This has given me a much greater appreciation for all of those cases of repressed memories that I have read about in recent newspapers and magazines.

♦ Feelings

Her words were calm and gentle, but it was not her words that were having the most impact. Beyond the words, were very intense feelings that seemed to rearrange my usual way of processing information. While I did not feel physically different, I cannot explain what it felt like, because there is no counterpart of words that would make any sense.

Real Feelings

Even though her words and explanations appeared unusual, it was my feelings that seemed more unusual because they were apparently being fine-tuned to process this experience.

She smiled at me and said, "You are just experiencing some of the real feelings that you were temporarily disconnected from because of a choice you made during a brief moment of curiosity. How you are feeling at this particular moment is your more natural way of experiencing."

Something in me knew what she meant because I didn't have an impulse to question her about anything at that particular moment.

Her voice was so soothing and so very disarming. I could only feel deep love and respect for her and from her. Her magnetism was so powerful.

Real Feelings

At the present moment, I am fully aware of the wisdom of feeling. Astrid taught me that what we usually refer to as feelings has more to do with emotions. She said emotions just cloud issues and have nothing to do with *Reality*.

These other feelings have more to do with what precedes thought. Whenever I stay aware of my feelings and then notice a thought, that one thought comes from the feeling at the center of how I am experiencing myself in that present moment. If I *really* know who I am in this present moment, then that feeling will foster the thought that supports that knowing awareness.

If I see myself as One with the totality of All That Is, my experiences will be based on the feelings of that knowing awareness. This is perhaps confusing because of the way we have been taught to view ourselves in relation to *Oneness*.

Real Feelings

When we view ourselves as outside of, or separate from, *Oneness*, we will see ourselves only as separate from everything else. Consequently, when we feel separate, we will experience the effects of separateness.

Probably all that I know about this today was planted in my unconscious awareness by Astrid in 1954. It was not until 1993 that I started to be aware I had that *knowing* awareness that Astrid mentioned.

♦ Be The Experience

Every one of the experiences I was given was necessary to remove each and every doubt. Believe me, there were plenty of doubts I had to let go. I was being reminded of who I really was by the inner feelings of my One Self. This is not unusual to me; everyone who pays attention to that quiet little voice within will have these same feelings and experiences. We just need to experience these feelings fully and *Be* the experience.

When I say, "*Be* the experience," I mean we let the experience expand without any analysis to find meaning or understanding. As soon as we begin to analyze what we are experiencing, the experience ends. If we need to analyze, we must wait for the experience to run its course.

From 1992 to 1994, I had many experiences in which I put this to the test. I do not have any doubt about the wisdom of *feeling*.

As awareness of these experiences expands, calmness, peace, and gentleness enfold all of our activities. When this becomes a habit, nothing outside of our inner awareness can affect us. The *knowing* that is present is the most powerful feeling of self-esteem. It allows the awareness of our *Real Self* to be present.

This experience gives one a whole new picture of what I call existence and what our *true* relationship is to one another. Perhaps you could say that it is the ultimate experience of *Love*. Unless one has this experience, words will not adequately convey this feeling of *Wholeness* and *Oneness*.

♦ True Beingness

Astrid told me that when a significant number of people start embracing the awareness of their feeling selves, we will then experience an upbeat generation of *True Beingness.*

"Upbeat?" I questioned.

"Yes", she said, "because this vibrational force of existence will begin to feel like it has been elevated to a higher level. It will resemble what you refer to as *Heaven on Earth.*"

I asked Astrid if she could reduce how we get to that point to one word.

"Absolutely—*feel*!"

She indicated that *feeling* was the one and only thing we ever needed to do, because everything else would take care of itself.

♦ Love

"What about love?" I asked.

"When you are *feeling*, what you are really doing is engaging in *Love*," was her reply.

Real Feelings

"Astrid, could you please tell me more about Love? When you use that word, it has a totally different feeling about it than what I am ordinarily used to," I queried.

"*Love* is not the same love you have been used to expressing, because there are too many conditions to what you call love," she stated. "Love is not something that you do in the back seat of a car," she stated with a big grin. "Incidentally, love is not a pit you fall into or a turnip truck you fall out of," she joked.

Her smile widened, and I immediately felt the Love she was expressing. Every cell in my body started to sing a song of absolute joy and contentment. Although I could not see my body, I bet it was glowing from this incredible experience of pure unconditional love. The Love was not being expressed to only one part of me, it was to the totality of my being. Wow! How could sex be better than that?

"Just what would you teenage boys think about all day long if you did not have sex?" she joked.

I knew at that specific moment I would have traded just about anything for that *Real feeling* of Love.

As a teenager, I did think a great deal about sex, but this experience was totally different. Although there were no sexual feelings associated with this type of experience, it was better than what I had learned about sex up to that point.

Astrid told me that it was possible to feel Love at the cellular level without interruption. That thought just seemed too wonderful to anticipate or believe.

She implied that everything we attempt to do to bring pleasure into our lives is really done to relive an experience of *Love*.

We never seem to have any lasting satisfaction because of our suspicion that something is really missing, but we do not remember what it is. Obviously, it is not something available in what we see. The implication is that there is a *knowing* within if only we would pay attention to it.

♦ Filling The Void

Why did it take me almost fifty-eight years of life to have that *Real experience* Astrid told me about when I was only eighteen years of age? I hope the youth of today is paying attention to this. The reward in self-esteem would be well worth it.

Real Feelings

We seem to search and search to find that *something* to fill an empty void that we know is there. The filling of this void is accomplished by merely listening and paying attention to the quiet voice of our *Real Self.* The answers that come from this listening will always be satisfying to whatever is needed.

How is this done? Astrid said that we can start by turning off the din that seems to grab our attention, and begin to feel—really feel—the *heart light* of our inner *Self.* Is this easy to do? Apparently not, but then again, she said that any excuse will do.

It is so easy to postpone doing the only thing that will bring lasting happiness and joy. Why? Astrid said it was simply because there was another voice that wanted our full attention, and that voice is at its full volume. The name of that other voice is ego.

Real Feelings

How do we turn down the volume? First, we must start by engaging in tranquil activities. These are activities that nourish our soul—contemplation, nature walks, looking into the eyes of a child, meditation, looking into a mirror and loving what we see, and the like.

Second, we can really join with another and see beyond the appearance of the body. There is a *heart light* just waiting for our acknowledgment within everyone we see, and that same *light* is also within all things that we see.

Third, we can begin to love everyone and everything we experience unconditionally. No matter the appearance, we can decide to see and embrace everything as acceptable—acceptable as Love.

Fourth, we can pay attention to our *feelings* about everything that we may encounter and "listen" for a message of the full acknowledgment of our equality.

Astrid indicated that these four things may be a good start to the awakening of the awareness of Love. With that awareness we may find that our experiences will begin to blossom into something *Real.* When the blossom opens, the *Light* will shine and brighten what used to be darkness.

♦ Excitement And Adventure

"How much excitement and adventure do you want in your life?" she inquired.

"After spending all of these years working hard in school, some excitement and adventure sounds real good," I replied.

"What are you really willing and able to give up in order to have this kind of stimulation?" she asked.

"If you mean money, I have none, but if you mean time, there is plenty of that," I responded.

"Time and money have no lasting value," she stated.

Astrid continued, "There is only one thing of value that you give up in order to participate with this stimulating 'drug' called excitement and adventure. You give up your awareness of *Self*, for that is all you really have of value. When you look for excitement, you get a certain amount of stimulation from the adventure."

"Do you really mean that a little excitement and adventure is a drug?" I asked.

"Yes!" Astrid pronounced. "This limited stimulation begs for a bigger and bigger 'fix.' That is why I called it a drug. You somehow think that you could be satisfied with just a little bit of stimulation; however, once tasted, the senses crave more and more. The reason you want more is because what you just received was not totally satisfying. It will never seem satisfying no matter how much excitement and adventure is attempted. This is one of the biggest enticements of illusion.

"I will speak of this later, but for now let me say it is part of 'seek but do not find.' It wants you to believe that you deserve some excitement in your life as a reward for all of your hard work. It would appear that a reward would offer some real value to you. Just the opposite is true. What poses as a reward only robs you of the awareness of *Self.*"

She then said, "Instead of looking for stimulation in adventure and excitement, one could be looking for it in the form of service to others. Being of service to others sounds so spiritually uplifting. This is not meant to infer that reaching out to others is wrong. If we want to be of service because we see others as needy, we can only engage in the validation of appearances. How is this of service?

"We must be very honest with ourselves with this. Are we reaching out to others because of a recognition of our *Oneness*, or are we seeing others as less than who they really are?

"Another side of this is being of service as a need to validate our own worthiness. In this case, we are seeing ourselves as less than who we really are. There are many subtle aspects to worthiness."

♦ Death And Judgment

"Is there actually any kind of life after death, Astrid?"

"First of all, my brother, there is no actual death. In this world, as you perceive it, there are many appearances that seem real; however, none of these appearances is real. All appearances are illusion; however, the *Love* underlying appearances is *Real.* When I say *Real,* I only refer to what is free of illusion. The *Real Self* is totally free of illusion. *Oneness* is free of illusion. *Love* is free of illusion. Nothing that you experience outside of your *Real Self* can have any effect. It may appear to have an effect, but appearances are all illusion."

Astrid elaborated, "What happens when you judge any of the appearances? Clearly, you can only engage in foolishness. Everything that is expressed and witnessed is subject to the perceptions of the one expressing and the one who is witnessing. I dare say there are no two people who view anything the same way. Each person has his or her own preconceptions of what anything means. Even the same person doesn't always see everything consistently.

"So if one person sees something one way and the another sees it differently, who is correct? When we judge one as being right and the other as being wrong, is our judgment valid? Apparently not, because there is no way anyone can make a judgment without having the complete history of everyone and everything involved in the decision since the very beginning of time.

"Do you know anyone with that ability? All this is being presented to point out the very foolishness of judging anything. In *Reality* any judgment is impossible simply because *Oneness* is already complete."

"Does this really have anything to do with life after death?" I asked.

"I am not really departing from your question," she said. "How is death viewed if one believes in reincarnation, in heaven and hell, in purgatory, in ascension, and so forth? Death can be viewed in many ways. Death is assigned whatever meaning we give it. So, from that standpoint, what is death?

"In contrast, *Oneness* cannot have any lessening of Itself. If it were really possible for anything to die, what would happen to *Oneness*? Do you see how absurd this is?

"Perhaps we could say that when someone appears to die, their appearance is removed from the awareness of each perceiver. This is done in various modes of acceptability. There are some people who still see some form of the departed, as there are those who go through endless grieving. Would you care to judge either one as right or as wrong? I will say that there is no actual death. If death were real, I would not be here with you. I will leave it up to you to accept that or to not accept it."

It was difficult for me to see another side that would contradict her view; however, I was wondering about the consequences of believing there was no death.

In my Catholic training, I was told that, aside from Purgatory, we ended up in Heaven or Hell upon death. If death did not actually happen, how do we get to heaven or hell, I was wondering? I also wondered how God fit in with this point of view.

♦ God

"If there is actually no real death, Astrid, what can you say about God?" I inquired. "There must be another way to reach God to get our reward without the necessity for death?"

"God—or not God—is not the reward or a punishment one gets for dying," she answered. "The way humanity sees this could be fodder for a good comedy routine. Who or What is God, you may be wondering? God is not a Who or a What—God Is! In fact, you could state your question in another way—'What is not God?' That would produce a very simple answer—nothing! I know you have the belief that God is present everywhere and in everything. Again, that is your belief, but it is not what you *Know.* When what you believe is replaced with *Knowing*, then you will not wonder about God.

"You also have the belief that God made you in His image and His likeness. That is just another 'speculation' you express without the tiniest sense of *feeling* what that really involves. You endlessly recite these beliefs without ever bothering to really listen to what you are saying. I will tell you that it is absolutely certain that God is present everywhere and as everything, including you. Did you hear what I just stated? INCLUDING YOU!

"If I say to you, 'Who are you, really?' can you give me an answer that would incorporate the whole truth without feeling guilty about your answer?"

"I am not really prepared to give such an answer at this time." I stated.

"You are not prepared to do that due to a conditioning in unworthiness," she answered.

"How can you possibly say you believe what you are professing to believe and feel unworthy? What could you be unworthy of in any sense of the word? Is it possible that you do not really believe what you profess, or is there some other reason?

"In spite of all of these questions, this is not any kind of interrogation. Do you see any rubber hoses or any bright spotlights?" she joked.

"You started to get a very serious look on your face," she said, "so I just needed to bring you back to the joyful and happy encounter this is supposed to be."

For the life of me, I just could not imagine Astrid ever using any interrogation tactics, and I started to laugh to such an extent, that I faded away for just an instant.

Real Feelings

I wondered why I should feel unworthy. How could I be unworthy if God is present in every part of me? Perhaps, I just need to start *feeling* God in each part of what I call me. If I could not do that, I would have to accept the fact that I felt unworthy at some level of my awareness.

What then came to mind was the possibility of another reason as suggested by Astrid. I recalled her saying that there was another voice vying for our attention—the ego. Why would this ego not want me to really believe what I was professing to believe? What power could the ego have over me? Perhaps, I needed to know more about this ego.

♦ An Experience With Mary

In 1993, I had an experience that demonstrated my feeling of worthiness.

I had heard Jesus state that the greatest thing His Mother Mary ever did for Him was to remind Him often that He was divine. Is it possible that we are here only to remind each other of our reality? Jesus stated that it was not too late for everyone to do the same thing for one another. In order to have this extraordinary experience with Mary, I hunted for my baby picture so I could really get into it. After finding the picture and studying it, I then went into a meditation and asked Mary to hold me as she would hold her own divine baby and to express to me what She really felt.

The first ten times I did it, I cried like a baby because I felt so unworthy to be in such a situation. She was very patient with me. On the eleventh try, I began to really feel Her love and gentleness. Her words were very soft and soothing. I could *Feel* the essence of my being actually responding to Her assurances of my birthright.

If anyone ever feels unworthy, I recommend this exercise, which should remove all doubt. We are much more than the appearances of the world suggest. Sometimes we just need to step out of our self-imposed comfort zones and allow these *Real Feelings* to come through. *Real Feelings* will give full meaning to comfort zones by changing our perception of what we see as limitation.

♦ The Ego

"Astrid, please tell me more about the ego," I implored.

She smiled and said, "My brother, you want me to tell you about something that does not really exist?"

Now I was really confused. I said, "You mentioned the ego voice earlier in our conversation, and indicated that it was a voice wanting our attention."

"Yes," she said with a wry smile, "I am making a point to which you should be paying very close attention. If I tell you the ego does not really exist, it is because it is only a part of what is called illusion. An illusion is a misleading image that is presented only to confuse your vision. The voice of illusion is strong whenever we give validity to appearances. We give validity to illusion anytime we react to anything suggested by an appearance.

"If the voice of the ego is only part of an illusion, how much of your attention should be given to it? It can yell and scream, but if you ignore its bleating, how effective of a leader will it be for you?

"A fantasy can be quite convincing while you are participating in it. After all, you may think that only a fool would deny the appearances. When you fully *Know* who you are, all of the appearances of the illusion, including the ego, will have zero impact. Is it the ego that is keeping you from really believing the truth, or is it your willingness to listen to its call with rapt attention?

"What if you placed your focus on what you are instead of what you are not? If you are not an ego, why should the ego be the center of your focus? Instead, place your full awareness on the *One* that you are. The solution is very simple, isn't it?"

♦ Simplicity

"I will now state another absolute truth—all real answers simplify! If the answer to any question seems complicated, refuse to accept it until it is reduced to simplicity. When you ask a question to that quiet little voice within, the real answer will be immediate and very simple. If the answer struggles to get out and it seems complicated, it will be from the fantasy world of the ego. The more you struggle with complications, the more time you will spend with the ego in an illusion. Whenever you use the brain to decipher any of these complicated answers, you will stay mired in illusion. That is really what the brain is for—to solve puzzles and you seem to like the challenge."

♦ Using The Brain

Astrid continued, "There are no puzzles in *Reality* because everything is simple. Does this mean that we don't need a brain in *Reality?* First of all, I want to point out that brain and Mind are not really the same. There is only one Mind, and it is shared by the *Oneness* that is us. A brain appears localized within an individual to solve puzzles. If there are not any puzzles to solve, why is there need for a brain? A brain processes the food for thought."

Astrid then said, "Here is the next shock for you—there is nothing to think about in *Reality*. Thinking is not Being! Doing is not Being! Being is Being! *Being* is happening in this present moment called *Now*. Nothing is happening aside from, or in addition to, *Being* in this present moment of *Now*. *Being* is the participation in the movement of *Love*. What we call *Oneness* is the total of that which participates *simultaneously* in this movement of the present moment referred to as *Now*. If nothing else can happen, thinking cannot occur. Truly, if thinking cannot happen, why would you need a brain? Is that too simple for you, my brother?

"If you want it to be more complicated, you can still remain under the influence of the ego in what seems like very familiar territory," she suggested.

"During the next forty years, you will become very familiar with all aspects of illusion. Your brain will seem to get a good workout. Since it is only illusion, none of this will be reflected in red ink on your permanent school record," she chuckled.

"It is interesting to listen to the speculation of your scientists who claim that individuals are only using a tiny portion of their brain. There is an implication that more of the brain should be used to solve problems. Quite the opposite is required. Less of the brain should be used in favor of *feeling*.

Real Feelings

"There seems to be a lot of concern about the so-called 'brain-dead' in your world. Perhaps a little more concern should be for the 'feeling-dead.' In 1994, you will stand up and be counted among the aware. It will catch you off guard; but once realization takes hold, nothing will ever be puzzling for you again."

"Can you give me a small hint of that 1994 incident?" I pleaded.

"If I do, how will you really be off guard?" she quipped.

When Astrid stated that I would stand up and be counted among the aware, she was correct. In March of 1994, I stood up at a presentation, and to my utter amazement, I stated that I was The Presence of Love, and that I was there to express Love. After I made the statement, it seemed appropriate.

♦ Inner Peace

"Can you tell me anything about how my life will be during the next forty years?" I begged. "Will I be rich? Will I find the love of my life? Will I be famous?"

"Is this what you really want to know about?" she whispered. "Haven't you grasped the gist of what is really important? Five years ago you filled out a questionnaire in which you indicated that your number one desire was inner peace. If that truly is your desire, what difference does it make what happens during the next forty years?

"I will tell you, my brother, even though you voted for inner peace, you certainly will not act like you want it. Instead, you will be searching for self-love. You will not be aware of that search until events seem to reduce you to a love-starved wretch. You will earnestly seek for some kind of fulfillment in a desperate attempt to be at peace.

"Consequently, you will really begin your search for what is truly missing from your awareness. You will eventually discover the *love* that is you, which will lead you to the *love* that is everything. At this moment you may be complaining about the necessity of it taking a long time to 'get with the program'; however, in the grand scheme of all things, it is only a very, very small moment."

Astrid continued, "Sometimes results are not appreciated when they appear to be easily attained. This does not mean that any struggle is necessary or recommended. Let me say that in your case, everything will be appropriate. I know this brief overview is not satisfying your curiosity, but I recommend that you let it be acceptable as stated. Will you let this be acceptable, my brother, or do we need to break out the rubber hoses again?"

(Our laughter must have stopped the world for at least a few moments.)

I guess it really didn't make any difference how much I knew about my life, if I was not going to remember any of this conversation until much later in life. It was just difficult to resist the temptation of asking questions. I guess we all have a tendency to want to know the future. Astrid seemed pleased with my acknowledgment of acceptance.

This, of course, is only my judgment of her reaction. Actually, I never did see Astrid react to anything in the usual sense of the way I reacted to anything, nor did I ever see her make any judgment to indicate that I was less than her in any way. Her manner was always kind and gentle.

When I was thirteen years old, I did fill out a questionnaire with some of the children in my neighborhood. The object was to reduce a short list of about twenty alternatives to one overall desire. It took about an hour to come to a decision. I did select inner peace as my life's number one desire. The fact that Astrid knew about that was a little unsettling. It made me wonder if everything we do is being carefully watched, judged, and then catalogued for use in the future. What came to mind was the final judgment day.

Astrid told me there are no private thoughts, but what we do is never judged at all. If our thoughts are not private, we must have full access to all thoughts. That would mean we are truly connected as one being.

♦ Reacting To Situations

"I am more than a little bit curious about how we should be reacting to any situation, Astrid."

"When you consider that you are only reacting to an illusion, doesn't that make you want to roll on the floor and laugh?" she chuckled. "Whenever you do react, you must be responding to a perceived stimulus. If there is really nothing outside of you, where is the stimulus with which you are responding? Actually it is nowhere! So, you may want to ask yourself why are you responding to a mirage."

She then stated, "When someone offers you an obscene gesture, you usually respond by displaying your own obscene gesture. You may ask yourself during this exchange of gestures, 'What am I really feeling as a result of this one reaction?' Chances are that you are feeling a tight knot in the pit of your stomach, which may be followed by a sensation of rising heat and then a most foul verbal explosion. Then off you go! Why? It was because you choose to react to something that was not there. Can you think of anything more insane than that?

"No matter what kind of situation, whatever seems to be going on around you can only be an expression of *Love.* If you don't see *Love,* you are engaging in some form of fear, which you are exchanging for *Love.* I must say, that is not an even exchange no matter how you evaluate anything. Everything that is *Real* responds from *Joy.*

"If you must react, a more peaceful and joyful response from you to the aforementioned obscene gesture could be laughter. You could force yourself to laugh by seeing the gesture differently. Could you look at the raised finger, laugh, and say to yourself, 'Ah, you recognize our oneness?' *Joy* would be present, and I'll bet you would not have a knot in the pit of your stomach. Also gone would be the rising heat and the verbal explosion.

"You always have a choice. You can react by engaging fear, or you can smile within yourself by acknowledging *Love* and *Wholeness*. You also would quit the judgment of what you thought was an attack in favor of a chance to laugh at a very humorous situation."

She added, "When you can see all that you have to do to be peaceful is to look for a loving response to any situation, you will not continue to judge what you are not really capable of judging. Isn't this a good enough reason to just laugh?"

♦ Brother And Sister

"Astrid, you have referred to me as your brother. Are you really my sister, or are you using the word 'brother' in another way?" I inquired.

She almost giggled at my inquiry before she said, "How do you view a sister, my brother?"

I could not help laughing at her question. It just struck me as funny trying to view Astrid as my sister. "A brother and his sister would probably have the same parents, and therefore be related," I suggested.

"Oh, we surely are related," she chuckled, "but we have really only one parent."

"Does that mean you are my stepsister?" I blurted out. She was gone for a long time. I guess my answer was very humorous to her.

"You have stated that you believe you were made in the image and likeness of God," she reminded me again. "Yet, you again demonstrate that it is still only a very weak belief or theory. If you were made in that wonderful way, why do you deny my existence coming into realization in the same manner? If we were each created in that same manner, how many parents do we have? I will answer this for you—One! Accordingly, what is our relationship to each other?

"Before you search for an answer, let me just add another crucial bit of information. It is something you have heard before, but like everything else you find difficult to comprehend, you just let it slide by. There is only ONE! Now, what is our relationship to each other, and what is our relationship to our Parent? It is difficult to find an appropriate word, isn't it? We will cover this soon, but for now, let me add that in *Reality* we do not use words. When I call you brother, I am being very polite in using a word you have familiarity with to give a hint of our relationship. We are not physically brother and sister; however, we are spiritually one and the same."

"Thank you," I responded, "that is one of the most beautiful and profound explanations that I have ever heard. I suppose that means we are truly soul mates in the absolute sense of that term, Astrid?"

"Absolutely!" she replied, "except the word 'mates' implies more than one. It is impossible for us to be more than *One.* It is also impossible for us to be less than *One*, as well."

♦ Words

"You said there are no words in *Reality*. If we do not use words, how do we communicate?" I asked.

"What is it you want to communicate?" she inquired. Immediately she added, "To communicate implies that something must be added to get some clarification or to make a connection. In *Oneness* everything is in place and everything is already connected. Likewise, there is no space or separation between anything that needs any filling. From your experiences, this is very difficult to imagine. One day you will have an experience that will clarify this and remove those doubts you now harbor. Until you have that experience, this subject will be very difficult to embrace."

"You are correct again, Astrid, because my brain just went into 'boggle mode' trying to imagine not using any words," I voiced. In 1994, I did have the experience Astrid foretold that removed all doubt about her assertion, which at the time was beyond my comprehension. (Author's note: This experience is detailed in my first book, *Please Remind Me I am The Presence of Love.*)

Astrid added, "Everything in your world is defined by the meaning you have given it. You may recall what I said earlier about the foolishness of judging anything. First, you define a thing by giving it the meaning you want it to have, and then you act as if it was defined by someone else. Each time you interact with a thing you defined, it is then saddled with your meaning.

"Incidentally, you call that communicating. You start talking about a thing as if it really *is* its definition. It is then catalogued in what you call a dictionary as a rule to follow.

"I will remind you, there is only *Oneness.* When that idea catches on, you will then realize that you have taken the one and only thing there is, and called it by millions of different names and have done so in many different languages. This seems innocent enough until you realize this is just another way of fostering separation. Anything that is done to honor separation is not appropriate.

"The more you try to separate, the more separation seems normal and believable. There is no brain to think with, no thoughts to think, no thoughts you have to communicate to anyone; and, therefore, zero words to use. I will also mention there is nothing boring or dull about being brainless, and we are not zombies."

(We both laughed uproariously at the stiff zombie image.)

♦ A Daydream

"My wonderful sister," I offered, "you indicated that we made a choice during one moment of curiosity not to experience our *Real Feelings*. Could you tell me more about that moment of decision and why we would want to do such a thing?"

"Thank you for recognizing me as your sister," she remarked. "You have an expression, 'Curiosity killed the cat, but satisfaction brought it back.' Even though your curiosity did not kill you, it did cause you to engage in what we will call a daydream that appeared to allow you to forget who you really are in *Truth*. You simply were curious about separateness.

"Since you didn't just laugh that curiosity away, the daydream was then projected out into what is called illusion. The instant you realized that separation was not for you, satisfaction brought you back to your awareness of *Self.* This all appeared to occur in a brief moment—from beginning to end.

"The daydream is really over, but you are just drifting back to that point of realization. When I tell you nothing that appears to be happening is actually happening, you think that I am just under the influence of delusion, or that I have been sniffing too much glue. I will be laughing with you at that point of this realization. In fact, everyone and everything will be laughing together at that point.

"Do not be surprised if the world just terminates in laughter. Perhaps you should start practicing laughter and get a head start on things. Isn't there an expression you have that states, 'Laugh and the world laughs with you'?

"You have had many experiences with daydreams while in your school classrooms. While distracted in these daydreams, you were not at all aware of the other students or even the classroom itself. Where did you go? You know that, while you didn't go anywhere, you were not aware you were still in the classroom. It seemed that you were elsewhere engaged in your fantasy. It was not until a sound, another student, or the teacher got your attention, that you returned to the awareness of the classroom.

"During these daydreams, it appeared that you were subject to all the consequences inherent in the fantasy you were having. Some of these dire consequences seemed so overwhelming to you. Yet, when you returned to the classroom in your awareness, you then discovered—thankfully so many times—that the so-called consequences had no real effect on you. You simply just became aware of where you had been all along. That is all that happened in this daydream you call life.

"The sound that is calling you back from this daydream is the sound of your own voice. We call that sound the quiet little voice within. Many refer to it as their guide, while others call it their intuition. It is actually who you really are—*Self*.

"Are you really beginning to listen? You will be amazed at what you will discover and *Feel* as you relax and let go of all preconceptions of what you think you are based on what the appearances of illusion tell you. The illusion is incapable of truth."

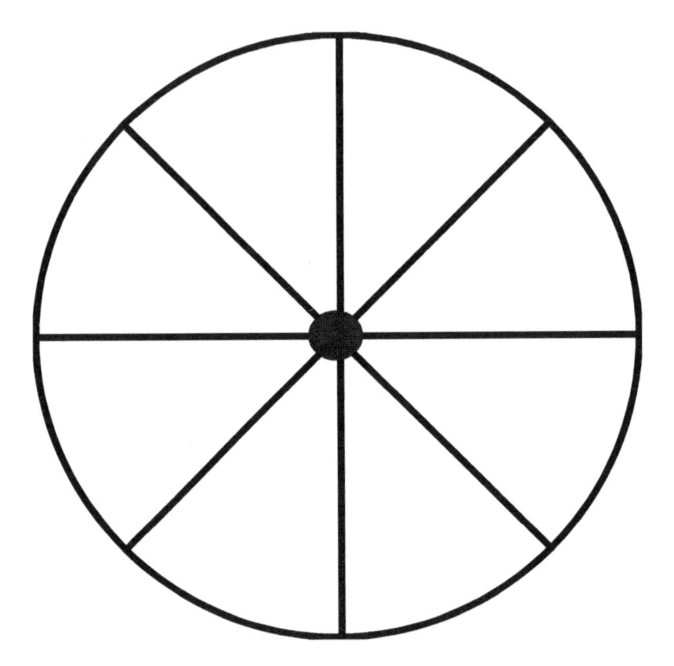

♦ The Wagon Wheel

"Perhaps I could clarify this a bit more with an illustration. When you look at a wagon wheel, you can see the spokes, the hub, and the outer rim. The hub will represent *Reality*, while the spokes can be seen as projections into illusion. You must realize that *Reality* has no form; but, for my demonstration, let us suppose that the hub really does represent *All That Is*. Anything outside the hub cannot be *Real*. I will call everything outside the hub 'illusion.' Another name for this illusion is appearances.

"When we wondered what it would be like to be separate, we engaged in a daydream that seemed to project us out from the hub into separate, distinct spokes. Please notice that the further one goes out on the spoke, the further one goes out from the hub, and the greater the separation between the spokes. The larger circle at the end of the spokes represents what we think is a finite universe.

"As we appear to move outside of the hub in search of answers to our puzzles, we seem to move further and further away from our center and from each other. In reality, we have never left the hub because we are only having the fantasy of a daydream.

"We set goals so we can accomplish something that we think will bring us success and happiness. We search for that perfect someone to live with happily evermore. Does any of that ever work out? Even the holiest saints seem to suffer. Instead of looking for answers 'out there,' the more prudent thing to do is to face the other direction and look within.

"It is so tempting to judge appearances. Whenever we do that, we get caught in the web of illusion and struggle to free ourselves from something that doesn't actually exist in reality. No wonder frustration seems so rampant in your limited awareness. The more we seem to struggle, the more we think there is something with which to struggle. We rationalize that if we are engaged in struggling, there actually must be something with which we are struggling.

"As we start to look within, we begin to *feel* the whispers of *Self* calling our awareness to attention. This awareness should begin to motivate us to stop the struggle and then 'head home.' As we move back to our awareness of *Self*, we begin to embrace more and more of the awareness of *Reality*. When we start to move toward the direction away from the finite universe of illusion, we begin to move a bit closer to each other. Consequently, we will not feel as separated from each other as we did before. I will call this particular movement 'relative truth.' Truth is always relative to what one can embrace in any given moment. As this awareness increases, more of this truth is revealed.

"As our awareness of *Self* expands, we then begin to let go of what we might consider our limitations. It is not possible for us to be limited in any way, except when our awareness is part of a fantasy. Again, I ask you, 'How can *One* be limited in any way?' If *One* could be divided into tiny fractions, each fraction would have to be present everywhere and as everything at the same time. Try to find a satisfactory explanation for that, my dear brother.

"As limitations drop, so does what these limitations hide—fear. *Love* cannot contain anything it is not. In illusion, fear appears to dilute *Love*. *Love* cannot be diminished by anything or anyone. I realize that appearances seem hypnotic, but once we begin to *feel* the *Love* that we are, the illusion will begin losing its grip in our awareness. As we embrace more and more of the awareness of *Self*, relative truth expands and becomes *Self*-awareness, which will then blossom into *Knowing.*"

♦ Consequences

"If it is really that simple, Astrid, and there are no consequences to what you call a daydream, why are there such fearful things such as Hell and a Devil?" I asked.

"Hey, it's your daydream. Why do you think you like to scare yourself with these incredible monsters?" Astrid answered. "Just look at your stories and your movies that are filled with all forms of gore designed to scare the hell out of you. Actually, you have gone one step beyond to scare the hell *into* you.

"Again, the simple answer—there is only *Oneness*. That means there is only *One*, which is pure *Love*. How can it be possible to have an opposite of *Love* coexisting with what is not *Love* in *Oneness*?

"You 'people' seem to like everything 'New and Improved'; maybe we could modify *Reality* and call it 'Oneness Plus'."

(Astrid exploded into great gales of laughter.)

"Sorry, my brother, that was even too funny for me. I hope you see the point. You asked a question that included a truthful statement that indicated there are no real consequences, which you followed with a statement containing consequences. It would indicate that you have not really accepted the 'no consequences' provision of what you say you believe. I hope you, too, are having as much fun with this as I am having."

"Yes," I said, "I have never had a teacher just like you. Perhaps you could provide my teachers with lessons in joy. Maybe you could free them up so they would not be so upset about every little thing that appears to go wrong. If learning is supposed to be fun, it must come from a happy teacher."

"Please pay close attention to all of your questions," she continued. "Your questions appear to belie your beliefs. This is actually helpful, because it forces you to be so very honest with yourself. Eventually you will believe what you say you believe; then you will move past that to *Know* what you say you believe. When you arrive at that point, you will not need any more beliefs or faith. Beliefs require evidence, whereas, faith implies certitude without any evidence. *Knowing* removes all doubt. When all doubt is gone, your full awareness will engage in *Being*.

Real Feelings

"Is there somebody against whom you harbor any hurtful feelings?" Astrid inquired.

"Of course," I replied, "Isn't that normal?"

"It is normal as long as you believe in appearances." she responded. "In the terms of *Reality*, whatever you think you hold against another, you actually hold against yourself. This illusion is fueled with the idea of a scapegoat upon which we can then project these unloving thoughts."

"What about people like Hitler and other tyrants?" I asked. "Aren't he and these others appropriate candidates for unloving thoughts?"

"Whenever we try to place someone outside our embrace of *Oneness*, we also must place ourselves outside," she emphasized. "When we really believe there is only *Oneness*, we will be fully aware that everyone and everything is included—without an exception. Hitler was just a very elaborate negative form for projection to give illusion more validity and thus justify fear and hatred."

♦ Becoming Spiritual

"How high of a mountain do you think one has to climb to be spiritually enriched?" Astrid queried. "Do you believe that the top of these mountains are reserved for the most holy of believers? There is a supposition that total denial of all material pleasures, as well as some self-flagellation, is required to be able to attain spiritual fulfillment. Suffering as a martyr is rewarded with sainthood in some religious circles. This may leave a strong message that suffering must be good for the soul.

"There is also a school of thought that says there are lessons to learn and steps one has to take to purify oneself. Supposedly, we are to look at each of the negative things that happen in our life and attempt to find some valuable lesson. These lessons are intended to prepare us for future holiness or sainthood, I suppose. All they actually do is keep us distracted and focused on the illusion.

"As we move up 'the spiritual ladder,' our lessons will appear to become more profound. Each step up is intended to prepare us for a deeper and richer understanding of our spiritual nature. This, of course, implies that all of these experiences are actually happening to us.

"Since this is all illusion, why do we have to do anything to earn what we already have? We have been given the fullness of Creation. The idea that we have to earn our way back to where we never left is ludicrous, at best.

"The only one that would engage in a journey of this sort is someone who did not know where he or she was already. This speaks volumes about the effectiveness of what appearances really do and our susceptibility to its enchanting siren song.

"As long as we pay attention to this idea that we are not already worthy of the abundance of Creation, we will continue to play this game of 'seek but do not find.' Isn't it interesting that the word 'seeker' is used to describe those who are on the so-called path of spiritual enlightenment? Where is this great 'finder' of this spiritual enlightenment? Perhaps one should just consider embracing the *Truth of Reality* and quit the seeking."

♦ Wealth

"How wealthy do you think you are, my dear brother?" Astrid inquired.

"That has got to be a joke," I responded. "I live in a low-income housing project unit on Suffolk Street with my parents and eight siblings. Most of our clothing is second-hand, and I have been working in odd jobs since I was about ten years old. I do not have two nickels to rub together.

"Our neighbors believe that our family is destitute. We do have a bit of fun at my mother's expense with that one. When she calls me to supper, I sometimes will respond to her by saying something like, 'It is not my turn today, I ate yesterday.' I am sure some of these neighbors believe it to be true, and it is probably great table conversation for these people."

"Whether or not you can accept it in this moment, you are wealthy beyond your wildest imagination," she said with great emphasis. "Our real wealth is not based on the puny prizes of any ego accomplishment. Since you are *One Self* united forever with your creator, your abundance must be total. If it could be less than that, how could there be *Oneness*?

"Your only lack is in a perception of lack as a result of a belief in appearances. Seeing beyond the appearances by looking within will prove to be a most worthy endeavor. There is an expression, 'Seeing is believing,' but just the opposite is true.

"Nothing that provides for a body contributes to your worth. As difficult as it may be for you to believe, you are not the body that you think you are seeing in your mirror."

♦ The Body

"Do you believe that the body you see is who you are?" she probed. She then continued, "A body can age, decay, get sick, suffer, and eventually appear to die. If you are Eternal, and I assure you that you are, how is it possible for you to become less than the Eternal Being that you are in truth? You cannot! However, you could continue to engage the appearances conjured up in an illusion by looking for satisfaction in what you think you are seeing. That kind of false satisfaction is short lived. In the world of appearances, the body comes to a cruel end—ashes to ashes, dust to dust.

"After the dust settles, we may begin to engage in some speculation about the whereabouts of the dearly departed's soul or spirit. Did it go on to its final reward or to further punishment, or worse yet, eternal damnation?

You are going to see just how pathetic this very strange view is before we are through.

"We are not the victims of some cruel joke. Instead, we appear to be willingly engaged in the fantasy that we have authored. Make no mistake about this, we are fully in charge of what appears as illusion. By using our free will, we only employ willfulness. This willfulness only causes the appearances of separation.

"In this dream state, we think that we are free to use a will that is different than the *One Will.* It is only a mistake in judgment in that we are judging the appearances as something valid. There are really no consequences associated with this mistaken judgment. If there were consequences, we would *all* have to share in them equally. After all, are we not *One?*

"We are not really subject to 'hell fire' or anything else that is less than the fullness of *Love* and *Wholeness.* Since we are eternally bound to be included in the *Oneness* of *All That Is,* the actual will that we really follow can only be the *One Will.*

"The idea that free will means a separate will is not the truth. When we look for the consistency in what we say we really believe, we will see what these appearances offer is complete insanity."

♦ Decisions

"There are no decisions to make, no goals to set or accomplish, nor is there anything or anyone to join," she emphasized. "Decisions imply a choice between alternatives. If *One* is all there is, and It moves in complete unity with everyone and everything, what other alternative decision can there be? When you think you see alternatives, you can only be seeing the appearances of illusion.

"Likewise, what does *One* have to join with to be more than what It is already? Furthermore, what goals can be employed to be in a more spontaneous union with this only possible movement? The *One Will* always moves in absolute unity as Itself. Seeing *Oneness* moving in many different directions at the same time is very amusing to envision, don't you think?

"When the full impact of the truth of these statements completely registers with your awareness, you will be finished with any need to question anything or anybody. In fact, you will not have the time for such questioning. Instead, you will actually *Be* the movement itself in the present moment."

♦ Control

"How much control do you think you can really exert over what appears in your awareness?" Astrid asked. "I will say," she then continued, "that control is something you will engage in whenever you think that you are in charge. You do not try to control any of those things that you think you are not in charge of. So, whenever you attempt any kind of control, you must actually believe you are in charge.

"That particular belief will keep you firmly tied to the appearances of an illusion. Does this really mean that you should be totally out of control? Yes, in the sense that you should try to exert any influence on what appears to be happening in illusion. Whenever you attempt to influence what is going on around you, you are placing that puny ego self in charge of this make-believe world. Is it any wonder you cannot find real satisfaction?

"All it really takes is a subtle shift in awareness to realize how foolish it is to have one aspect of an illusion trying to control a larger aspect of this illusion. Control is nothing more than willfulness. There is only *One Will*; however, when you attempt to control anything, you are saying, in effect, 'my will be done.' It is a decision to be separate where you can make judgments as to what is right or wrong. That is a lot of useless effort and it belies a belief in *One Will.*

"Whenever you decide something is not totally acceptable, you are then engaged in control. If you then let all things be acceptable, you will be acknowledging that you are not in charge. This acknowledgment will allow the *One Will* to be the fullness of your awareness and experience. The *One Will* cannot be changed, but your awareness can be."

♦ Holding On

"What are you holding on to?" she asked.

Before I could answer, she added, "Let go of whatever it is so you can see the absurdity of holding on to anything. Whatever you hold, only holds you. You cannot simplify your life if you carry the weight of the world on your shoulders. When you let go of everything you will feel a buoyancy or lightness that will set you free of attachments. This will be the beginning of the peace that is without understanding, but with *Knowing*.

"Say, for example, I put a large sum of money in a very large, heavy jar with a narrow neck that you could barely squeeze your opened hand into to reach the money. But say that you couldn't take your closed hand out of the jar, what would you try to do? You probably would think of many ways to get the money out without letting any of it get away. In the meantime, that attachment would hold you as a prisoner. Not only are you the prisoner, but you are also your own prison warden. You have decided to let that attachment be so much more important than what would be your freedom. You could just as easily open your hand to let the money go and gain your freedom, but at the moment freedom seems like too high a price to pay.

"What this illustrates is how you handle all of your attachments. When I say attachments, I include such things as judgment, anger, resentment, imagined wants or needs, as well as anything that you hold special. Letting anything go is really as simple as opening your hand to peace instead of holding on to any one of these attachments.

"You have had a recurring dream of finding coins. These dreams seemed so real to you that when you awoke in the morning, you could feel these coins clutched in your hand until you opened your hand to find nothing. Every attachment holds only an empty promise without ever having any hope of fulfillment.

"What I am suggesting to you is that you do not strive for attachments to anything or anyone. That also means to be totally free of any goals or desires. Am I suggesting that you just become irresponsible? Not at all! Just let what comes or does not come your way be acceptable just as it is. This is the way to be free of attachments. Just ask if what you are holding on to is worth it."

♦ Beliefs

I asked Astrid, "Who is more correct, the atheist who says that there is no higher power, or the other person who says there is a higher power?"

"They are both correct, but not for the reasons they think," she responded. "As I said, there is only *Oneness*, so that must mean there is no one above the one who is known as an atheist. Thus, the so-called atheist is one with everyone and everything. Maybe the atheist is not perceiving this unity as the reason for his position. The person who believes in a higher power has the conviction that something greater is beyond his limited concept of the ego self. That is correct, but he is also one with the higher power that, perhaps, his limited ego self just refuses to acknowledge. If he is really one with this power, how could it be considered higher?

Real Feelings

"It is so very convenient to judge one as right and the other one as wrong when they are both right but maybe for the wrong reason."

"If everyone could see things as you do, we would not have anything to argue about, and can you just imagine such a world?" I suggested.

"Since we are all *One*, the only one we can argue with is ourselves," she said.

"Have you ever considered running in an election for world leader?" I joked.

"Oh, my brother, we are already the leader of the world in *Reality*," she laughed.

Then she added, "Who can be the leader of *One*? Who can be the follower of *One*? Isn't this just a grand joke?"

♦ Male And Female

"Astrid, I appear to be a male, and you appear to be female, yet you insist that we are one. Isn't that a rather big contradiction?"

"It only appears to be a contradiction, just as you appear to be a male and I appear to look like a female," she responded.

Astrid then stated, "Appearances are truly very deceiving. Even though we *appear* different, we cannot, in reality, be different. The many appearances within the illusion are there to give the daydream validity. Every single thing you think you see is what the magician of illusion uses to convince you that what comes out of the 'smoke and mirrors' has truth and reality. A great magician can convince you of anything if you go along with his slight of hand.

This magician was conjured up in our own imagination as we wondered what it would feel like to be separate.

"We cannot try to look outside of ourselves to find someone to blame. We do have a choice—we can begin to laugh at our own bag of tricks, or we can take illusion very seriously. Which do you prefer? For many years to come, you will peek into the fun house mirror and play the game of hide and seek, until you are ready to accept *Truth*. The amount of laughter in your life will be a telltale sign of your readiness."

♦ The End Of Illusion

"When will we all catch on to this magic act, Astrid?"

"In terms of a calendar, the magic show will begin to lose its appeal around the turn of the next century," she predicted. "The pessimist in us will say that it will happen because of the fear of the millennium. Our more optimistic self will see it approaching as an outgrowth of a long-term inner dialogue with *Self.* Even though we may not immediately identify it as *Self, Self*-awareness is the only valid key to the awakening of awareness. *Self* will be called by many names that will include every so-called spiritually evolved personage who has ever existed or who has ever been imagined.

"Actually, there is only one reason why *Self* is not recognized early on—unworthiness. Why do I say it is unworthiness? Because, it seems difficult for us to include ourselves along side with, and equal to, all of these 'holy saints.' Nevertheless, worthiness will catch on. In fact, you will be one of the 'radicals' in the forefront of a most grand and magnificent spiritual revolution. This will not be a bloody revolution in terms of any past military operations or battles, but a very, very gentle and peaceful campaign that will be difficult, if not impossible, to ignore.

"Peace and Joy will be the only 'weapons' of choice. The intellectuals will be the last to be persuaded because they will find it difficult to put down their 'cannons' of logic or their canon of law, thought, and judgment. Simplicity will be too simple to grasp, but grasp it they will along with everyone else who appears as separate beings. This will be beautiful to watch, and we will watch it as *One*."

"Me a radical?" I exclaimed with a grimace.

"Not to worry, my dear brother," was her firm reassurance. "You will not

hard you may try. Of course, I am only joking about you being a poor student. You have grasped more than you now realize. Realization will come to you quite gently as you begin to awaken to the awareness of your real being. This awareness will provide the great *Light* that all will see.

"I am like a gentle signpost along the way that is just reminding you of who you really are. You will also be a reminder to those who seem as if they are separate brothers and sisters. You may have wondered why you were chosen. I will say to you, who else is there? Yes, again I am reminding you of *Oneness.*"

♦ Realization Of Self

"Astrid, when will I have the realization of who I am?" I inquired.

Real Feelings

Astrid replied, "Realization sometimes comes as a flash of awareness, and other times it seems like a slow awakening. You will go through many of what you will call 'spiritual guides' that will give you feelings of some very wonderful inspiration. These guides will include Jesus, The Holy Spirit, and several of the other so-called spiritual entities.

"So, what I am about to suggest is not to criticize anyone for engaging in subterfuge. There will come a point in your life where The Holy Spirit will tell you to accept who you really are by realizing The Holy Spirit and you are one and the same *Self*. At first you may find that really hard to accept. Your worthiness will take some time to catch up with this most wonderful possibility of *Oneness*. However, eventually you will accept that as *Truth* and the full realization of *Oneness* will dawn in your awareness."

Astrid then expanded, "Many individuals claim to be channeling Jesus, and many more say that Jesus is communicating with them. I have great news—it is not Jesus, it is *Self.* The appearance of the person who is referred to as Jesus is really just an appearance of an elaborate ego form. Apart from the form is the Christ Consciousness and only that is *Real.* To say that it is Jesus who speaks to or through us is only an aspect of a feeling of some lack of worthiness to be *One Self.* This can only be seen as a firm acknowledgment of separation.

"Whenever we acknowledge separation, we validate and prolong illusion. The next time anyone says they are communicating with Jesus, ask if there is any separation between the 'voice' that represents Jesus and one's *Real* voice. If the answer is that there is no separation, who is 'speaking' other than

Self? In contrast, if the answer indicates there is an actual separation, then illusion is being acknowledged as something real.

"One can also ask this 'voice of Jesus' if it is really the Christ Consciousness. If the answer is affirmative, the 'voice' must be *Self*. On the other hand, if the answer indicates that it is not the Christ Consciousness, then it can only be another aspect of ego, albeit in a fancier form of illusion."

She elaborated, "If I claim there is only One, how can I separate anything from me? To say that there is a Jesus apart from me is an acknowledgment of separation. Everything and everyone that can exist is who I am, and I call that *Self*. Whenever I feel unworthy enough to believe that I am not *Self*, I will then acknowledge 'higher forms' to do my speaking for *Self*."

Astrid then said, "I Am that I Am! There are no exceptions to that statement of truth," she continued, "other than when we feel unworthy to embrace it. I realize that 'unworthiness' is a very strong word; however, there is no better word to capture our attention and to clarify the situation.

"Do we feel worthy enough to be the same as Jesus? If we do not, then we must not be feeling worthy enough to be one and the same as Jesus, and that could only confirm separation. Could Jesus just be an ego ploy to keep us tied to illusion? As long as we want to see someone above us, our awareness will reflect that belief.

"Whenever we believe that Jesus is somehow elevated above us, we tacitly acknowledge separation. The moment we feel one with everyone and everything, there cannot be any separation.

In contrast, if we think that anyone or anything is above us, we must believe in separation.

"It may sound very spiritual to ask someone to channel Jesus, or to ask Jesus to speak to us. When we do that, what are we really saying? We can only be agreeing to acknowledge separation. Of course, we can still want to hear the beautiful pronouncements from Jesus, while at the same moment, acknowledging separation. We can try to convince ourselves that it is better to hear Jesus while we are feeling separate than to feel separate and not hear Jesus.

"There may also be a subtle form of one-upmanship by those who claim to be channeling or guided by Jesus or some other entity. When we realize this is just another ego trick, can we feel worthy enough to go directly to *Self* and bypass this sophisticated form of higher ego? The voice of *Self* may sound the same as the voice of Jesus, but the separation and unworthiness will be absent."

Astrid then asked, "How do we go directly to *Self*?"

"Please tell me," I implored.

She answered, "As we continually acknowledge *Oneness,* we will be 'praying without ceasing.' This is a continuous prayer that will be a reminder of *Wholeness.* This reminder will 'spark the *Light*' that will produce the *Joy. Self* will begin to laugh, and this laughter will blow away the fog of illusion."

♦ Heaven

"Is there a place called 'Heaven,' since there is apparently no place called Hell?" I said with a chuckle.

"When you say 'Heaven,' do you mean with the Pearly Gates, Saint Peter, and angels playing harps?" she joked. "There is no place with a sign that says, 'Entering Heaven, Population One, Established in Year One,' if that is what you mean. Remember I said we do not use words in *Reality*. Obviously, I am having a lot of fun with you about this. You, too, are going to arrive at the place where you are going to have fun with everything. Playing and laughing will become your natural behavior. When you catch on you will have much fun.

"Heaven, as you are perceiving it, does not exist. What does exist is everything and everywhere where you have always been. I have been calling this *Oneness*. However, I cannot really paint a picture of *Oneness*. How could I actually describe *All That Is* when it is *One?* How can I ever separate what cannot be separated into so many parts? Again, words are only for separating one into more than one. However, in this case, One would have to be separated into something less than One. That is why *One* simply *Is.*"

♦ Complication

Astrid stated, "There seems to be a very large problem in attempting to explain simplicity simply. Obviously, it is because words always complicate what is beyond being complicated. Thank God we do not have to use any words in *Reality!*"

(Astrid was engaged in a laugh-fest.)

"Do you see why any explanation can only appear to complicate simplicity? However, *Being* always allows complete freedom."

Astrid had such a marvelous way of simplifying the mystique surrounding what I had considered unassailable. No matter how very simple something is, it is impossible to reduce its simplicity by using words without complicating its very simplicity. I am left only with the opinion—why try to complicate it? By its very nature "trying" actually seems to add complication to the simplifying process itself. Perhaps I should only engage in simplicity and see what happens. I suppose that will make me simple-minded.

"I seem to be arriving at a point where I am beginning to wonder why I should even try to do anything at all," I speculated.

"Excellent, my brother!" was her retort. "Whenever we try to do anything based on the appearances of illusion, we prolong the illusion by engaging it.

"Just refuse to engage it. Instead, if we listen to our own inner voice by really *feeling* what I will refer to as 'guidance,' we will be navigated into the smooth waters of *Reality*. The ride in this pure water is without any effort or the use of a separate will. There really is nothing that we need to do to be in this peaceful state.

"Flow, flow, flow with the water gently in the stream," she sang.

Astrid then joked, "Isn't that better than being up the creek without a paddle? The latter is the way of the ego, whereas, the former is so very gentle and natural."

"Flowing gently in this stream sounds so much more peaceful than all that rowing. I just have to accept the fact that I really have nothing to do," I answered.

♦ My Feelings

"Well, my dear brother, what of this encounter has really registered with you in the way of true *feelings*?" Astrid probed.

"Of course, the most overwhelming thing that immediately comes to mind," I replied, "is the importance of what you called *feelings*. When it becomes possible for my awareness to accept more of *Self*, I will more fully comprehend the wisdom of your teaching. It is not as if I am going to part company with you and immediately become aware. You said that it will take about forty years before I will start to have awareness of anything that you have so beautifully described.

"Perhaps it is a real blessing in disguise that I will not remember any of this before I can become more patient.

Waiting patiently for forty years to go by sounds almost impossible. It seems like a waste, except for the awareness that this is all an illusion anyway. If only I could keep that perspective, I would become much more patient and be able to tolerate almost any situation that would present itself to me.

"That brings us to acceptance, because the patient person will not want to be honoring any of the appearances of illusion. Instead, the more patient person would not want to ever try to control anything or anyone. Likewise, the constant chattering of the ego would be ignored in favor of the awareness of *Self*. In particular, I would not be judging anyone without the full realization that I can only be judging myself. Therefore, whenever I am ever tempted to judge or want to react to anything, I could just see it as it really is and then laugh to myself.

"What comes to mind is the expression, 'I am going to laugh myself to death.' Since there is no real death, the death will be only that of illusion. You did say that this great awakening of awareness would arrive filled with much laughter."

I continued, "What I gather from your 'wagon wheel' analogy is that my only sensible choice is to stop looking into the fun house mirror for a reflection of reality. Instead, I should silently embrace *Oneness* and let it be my one and only experience. Gone will be any attempt to try to solve puzzles from the world of smoke and mirrors. Gone will be any need to find meaning or understanding in the fragmented figments of a daydream. As a result, I will not have to hold on to anything or anybody to establish my worthiness. In the *Wholeness of Reality*, I am the only leader as well as the only follower. If I cannot totally accept that, then I cannot accept *Oneness.*"

I elaborated, "My worthiness was established in the instant that I was created in the image and likeness of God. Truly, nothing can alter worthiness, unless I willfully disconnect my awareness from my *Real Source.* This is not possible to do, but we could engage in the fantasy of really thinking it is so. You say we do this when we cater to any illusion of separation. Thus if we do not honor illusion, it cannot touch us in any way.

"We even do this in seemingly holy ways by honoring the ploys of a most sophisticated ego. If we believe there is only *Oneness* and *Wholeness*, we must be consistent in how we honor that belief. No matter how very holy it appears, nothing can be separated from *Self.*

"Thus, if we discover that we are struggling with even this issue, the key is to be aware that any struggle constitutes illusion. *One* cannot struggle with *One!* As innocent and as holy as channeling may sound, it is still struggle. The main struggle is not obvious. It is really the nonacceptance of *Self* by the one claiming to be the channel that is the key issue. As soon as worthiness is accepted, the need for channeling will be over in favor of *Self*-acceptance.

"Whenever I am tempted to ask, 'Why me?' or to know why I was chosen, I am only forgetting the very simple answer—Who else is there? Indeed, I await the awareness of this brainless and wordless state of *Being* where I will just be content to 'go with the flow' that you speak about."

"Bravo, my dear brother!" Astrid exclaimed. "You probably are not really as stupid as you may appear. Perhaps I have not actually wasted my time with you after all," she said with very much laughter.

♦ The Real Focus

"At this point, you may be thinking that it is too bad you cannot come away from all of this with the full awareness that you think you now have," she said in reflection.

"I will be as frank as I can be in this," she went on. "Every time you express the slightest doubt about your *Real* identity, you will always seem to forget what is *Real.*

"I have repeatedly said that the daydream is illusion. That means that illusion cannot have any kind of validity. Illusion has never happened! Since it never happened, how can you have forty or so years to waste, or for that matter millions of years? As I said before, just focus on who you are, not on who you are not. With that focus, you will see clearly without any fog to cloud your vision."

♦ Returning To Illusion

Astrid gave me a look that indicated our brief encounter was just about finished. I felt that she had imparted whatever wisdom I needed to have for whatever purpose I needed to have it. Truly, I did not want this experience to end. The experience of peace and joy in this encounter was enchanting.

Apparently, it was now appropriate for me to rejoin the illusion of the human experience of walking back to my home from school.

The last thing I now remember of this wonderful experience is entering the shaft of the light that brought me aboard the craft. It was as if the experience happened the very moment my right foot hit the pavement and it was over as my left foot landed. My mind was still on graduation. This experience was as imperceptible as a single step in time.

Astrid was correct again about it seeming timeless. I was totally unaware that anything so very marvelous had just happened to me.

In retrospect, it was a step that eventually changed the course of my life. What now comes to mind is the statement by Apollo Astronaut, Neil A. Armstrong, as the first man to set foot on the Moon on that historic day in 1969: "That's one small step for a man, one giant leap for mankind."

♦ Under The Oak Tree

We were back under the oak tree in our awareness. Her smile was so very beautiful, and I felt so very content just to stay in that spot forever and bask in her joy.

"You think that forty-one years of life is a long time for someone to forget something?" she asked. "Yet when you heard my greeting, you remembered what was repressed. Similarly, when you started to listen to the voice of *Self*, you began to *feel* the *Truth* that you had tried to repress since the very beginning of time.

"Actually, any time is meaningless, whether it is one year or a million years, because time never began. The illusion of time began only as a fantasy which provided many appearances for you to engage. The instant realization dawns in awareness—poof—illusion will seem like it never happened. Now that you fully realize who you are, did the forty-one years really make any worthwhile difference in the grand scheme of all things?"

"No, not really," I responded. "It really doesn't matter what happened in illusion or how long it appeared to take. What is important to me in this moment is that I feel completely peaceful. The weight of the world is off my shoulders and I do not have to cater to ego fantasies again."

"That is correct, my brother," she agreed. "As you look at me now, you are really seeing *Self*. I am mirroring what you are allowing yourself to fully embrace. As the sureness of *Self* reaches out of time, you will *know* our lighted *Self* in its absolute pure state of *Joy* and *Love*.

"In that moment, under the oak tree, when I greeted you, didn't you immediately connect with the *feeling* of our previous meeting? In that connection, how much time passed in your awareness?"

I was stunned at her remark. In brief reflection, it was as if we had never been apart. Was this another one of the magician's tricks? Although it may have appeared that many different events occurred to me since that momentous May afternoon in 1954, nothing *Real* had happened.

"Astrid," I said, "how can this be? It is so confusing."

She just smiled, "You have already stated the only answer in your mind—nothing *Real* had happened. Yes, the daydream seemed to contain all of the appearances of something happening.

Do you not find this amusing? How could forty-one years be meaningless? However, when viewed from the perspective that it was illusion, what was meaningless? Only illusion is meaningless because it cannot happen. So, what was really meaningless? Are you as totally confused as you appear to look, my brother?"

"Actually, I am astonished at how easily and simply you state the obvious, while, at the same time, I feel so perplexed at my lack of understanding of simplicity," I meekly offered. Then, I added, "If everything is as simple as you infer, why do I seem to want to make it so much more complicated than it really is?"

"But, you have not," she beamed, "it is just that you keep forgetting who you are—that is all. You cannot change the *Truth* no matter how much illusion you appear to swallow. You are *One Self* fully united with *All That Is*. Any other opinion has no justification or any validity whatsoever. Just continue to see and honor who you really are, not who you are not.

"I am with you always, for it cannot be otherwise—*Oneness* is our nature. We are *One Self* forever."

With that final statement, Astrid smiled and then faded from my awareness. I was left with a total confirmation of the experiences of the last few years that certainly verified her great teaching of Joy in 1954.

Astrid removed the very last doubt I had about who I really am. I am The Presence of Love as is everything and everyone The Presence of Love.

"I am with you always,
for it cannot be otherwise
--Oneness is our nature.
We are One Self forever."

Astrid

About the Author

Brother Bob (Bob Wayman) was born in Lowell, Massachusetts, in 1936, the eldest of nine children. Being a brother seems so very natural to Bob. In his youth, he remembers completing a questionnaire asking for his ultimate goal. He chose *inner peace,* over such corporeal values as fame and fortune. He started his spiritual quest in 1974 because he was looking for meaning in his life. Bob explored many of the aspects of the spiritual adventure before becoming a student of *A Course in Miracles*® in 1982. In November 1990, Bob decided to turn all decisions over to the "Higher Self" instead of attempting to intellectually understand or do anything on his own. At that point, the world took on a different meaning, and peace and joy began to embrace all of his activities. Bob resides in Northern California with his lovely wife Cari and two kitties, Reno and Sparks.

His first book, *Please Remind Me I am The Presence of Love,* is available from the publisher,

HEAVEN